A+ books

POLAR ANIMALS

POLAR BEARS

ARE AWESOME

by Jaclyn Jaycox

Consultant: Greg Breed
Associate Professor of Ecology
Institute of Arctic Biology
University of Alaska, Fairbanks

PEBBLE
a capstone imprint

A+ Books are published by Pebble,
1710 Roe Crest Drive, North Mankato, Minnesota 56003
www.mycapstone.com

Library of Congress Cataloging-in-Publication Data
Names: Jaycox, Jaclyn, 1983–author.
Title: Polar Bears Are Awesome / by Jaclyn Jaycox.
Description: North Mankato, Minnesota: an imprint of Pebble, [2020] |
    Series: A+. Polar Animals | Audience: Age 4–8. | Audience: K to Grade 3. |
    Includes bibliographical references and index.
Identifiers: LCCN 2018056760 | ISBN 9781977108180 (hardcover) | ISBN
    9781977109989 (paperback) | ISBN 9781977108272 (ebook pdf)
Subjects: LCSH: Polar bear—Juvenile literature. | Animals—Polar
    regions—Juvenile literature.
Classification: LCC QL737.C27 J385 2020 | DDC 599.786—dc23
LC record available at https://lccn.loc.gov/2018056760

Editorial Credits
Nikki Potts, editor; Kayla Rossow, designer; Morgan Walters, media researcher;
Laura Manthe, production specialist

Photo Credits
Alamy: National Geographic Image Collection, 7; Dreamstime: Belovodchenko, 21; Newscom: Dennis Fast - VWPics, 20; Shutterstock: Alexey Seafarer, 28, BMJ, 15, Caleb Foster, spread 10-11, Chase Dekker, 18, DonLand, 12, EhayDy, 23, FloridaStock, 6, spread 24-25, Incredible Arctic, 8, jo Crebbin, Cover, Kostin SS, 16, Mara008, design element (blue), Mario_Hoppmann, 25, Mikhail Kolesnikov, 9, miroslav chytil, 29, Nagel Photography, 5, NaturesMomentsuk, 17, Oliay, design element (ice window), Ondrej Prosicky, 14, 27, outdoorsman, 4, photosoft, design element (ice), Rene Rasmussen, bottom 11, Sergey Uryadnikov, 19, 22, Vladimir Melnik, 26, vladsilver, 13

All internet sites appearing in back matter were available and accurate when this book was sent to press.

Note to Parents, Teachers, and Librarians

This Polar Animals book uses full-color photographs and a nonfiction format to introduce the concept of polar bears. *Polar Bears Are Awesome* is designed to be read aloud to a pre-reader or to be read independently by an early reader. Photographs help listeners and early readers understand the text and concepts discussed. The book encourages further learning by including the following sections: Table of Contents, Glossary, Read More, Internet Sites, Critical Thinking Questions, and Index. Early readers may need assistance using these features.

TABLE OF CONTENTS

Bath Time!

A playful polar bear rolls in the snow. It's taking a bath! Polar bears rub their wet fur in the snow after a swim. The snow helps them stay clean and dry.

Polar bears live in one of the coldest places on Earth. Dry fur helps keep them warm.

Big Bears

Polar bears are the largest type of bear. Males are about 8 feet (2.4 meters) long. They can weigh more than 1,300 pounds (590 kilograms).

Females are two to three times smaller than males.

Polar bears blend in with the white snow. But their fur is actually clear! Each hair is hollow and reflects sunlight. This makes the bears look white like the snow.

Polar bears have black
skin under their fur. It soaks
up sunlight and keeps them
warm.

9

Polar bears are excellent swimmers. They use their big paws to paddle. They have a thick layer of blubber. It keeps them warm in the icy water.

Polar bears have fur on the bottom of their feet. They also have large claws. Claws grip the ice and help polar bears walk on the slippery surface.

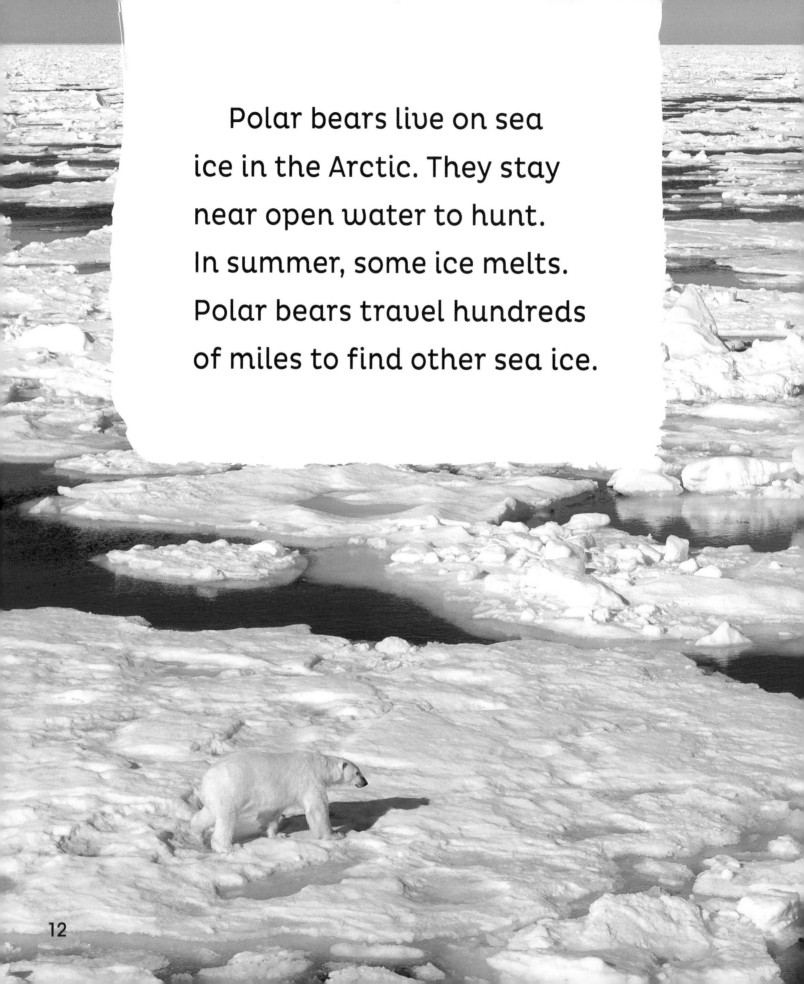

Polar bears live on sea ice in the Arctic. They stay near open water to hunt. In summer, some ice melts. Polar bears travel hundreds of miles to find other sea ice.

Some bears move to land. Polar bears can go without food for a few months until the water freezes again.

Finding Food

A hungry polar bear lies next to the water's edge. It waits. Suddenly, a seal pops up. *Snatch!* The polar bear has caught its dinner.

Seals are a polar bear's top prey. Polar bears also hunt walruses and beluga whales. Polar bears get water from the food they eat.

Polar bears have a strong sense of smell. They can smell a seal on the ice up to 20 miles (32 kilometers) away. They can even smell a seal's den under the snow. Polar bears eat the blubber of a seal. They can eat more than 100 pounds (45 kg) of blubber in one meal!

Family Life

Polar bears live on their own. They come together only to mate. Polar bears growl or hiss if they are threatened.

They also like to play
fight if they come across
other bears. They stand on
their back legs and try to
knock each other over.

Females build dens in the snow. Mother bears raise cubs in the dens. Most females have two cubs at a time.

Cubs are very small when born. They weigh about 1 pound (0.5 kg). Cubs don't have a lot of fur. Their mothers keep them warm while they grow. Cubs drink milk from their mothers.

Polar bear cubs come out of the den after about three months. They stay with their mother as long as three years.

She teaches them how to hunt and swim. Polar bears can live 25 years in the wild.

Staying Safe

Adult polar bears have no predators. But they face other dangers.

The changing climate is affecting them. Ice melts as temperatures rise. Polar bears need ice to hunt. With less ice, they may have a harder time finding food. Without food, they can't survive.

Oil spills are another threat to polar bears. Oil leaks out of boats traveling through Arctic waters. Oil sticks to polar bears' fur. Their fur can no longer help to keep them warm. If a polar bear gets oil on its fur, it will not survive in the cold Arctic.

There are about 26,000 polar bears on Earth. They are the biggest bears in the world.

They are also one of the toughest! Not many animals can survive in the Arctic. But it's the perfect home for a polar bear.

GLOSSARY

Arctic (ARK-tik)—the area near the North Pole; the Arctic is cold and covered with ice

blubber (BLUH-buhr)—a thick layer of fat under the skin of some animals; blubber keeps animals warm

climate (KLY-muht)—the average weather of a place throughout the year

den (DEN)—a place where a wild animal may live; a den may be a hole in the ground or a trunk of a tree

female (FEE-male)—an animal that can give birth to young animals or lay eggs

male (MALE)—an animal that can father young

mate (MATE)—to join together to produce young

polar (POH-lur)—having to do with the icy regions around the North or South Pole

predator (PRED-uh-tur)—an animal that hunts other animals for food

prey (PRAY)—an animal hunted by another animal for food

threat (THRET)—something that can be considered dangerous

READ MORE

Cooper, Sharon Katz. *A Day in the Life of a Polar Bear: A 4D Book*. A Day in the Life. North Mankato, MN: Capstone Press, 2019.

Marquardt, Meg. *Polar Bears on the Hunt*. Predators. Minneapolis: Lerner Publications, 2018.

Schuh, Mari. *Penguins*. Black and White Animals. North Mankato, MN: Capstone Press, 2017.

INTERNET SITES

National Geographic Kids, Polar Bears Profile
https://kids.nationalgeographic.com/animals/polar-bear/

Polar Bears International
https://polarbearsinternational.org/education-center/school-report-materials/

San Diego Zoo, Polar Bear: The Great Ice Bear
https://kids.sandiegozoo.org/index.php/animals/polar-bear

CRITICAL THINKING QUESTIONS

1. Where do polar bears live?

2. Polar bears have a thick layer of blubber to help keep them warm. What is blubber? (Hint: Use the glossary for help!)

3. What dangers to polar bears face?

INDEX